Biomes
of North
America
Second Editions

A Walk
in the
Desert

2nd Edition

by Rebecca L. Johnson

with illustrations by Phyllis V. Saroff

Lerner Publications ◆ Minneapolis

For Eric, lover of wild places and hot, dry climates

Lerner Publications Company
An imprint of Lerner Publishing Group, Inc.
241 First Avenue North
Minneapolis, MN 55401 USA

For reading levels and more information, look up this title at www.lernerbooks.com.

Main body text set in Garth Graphic Std.
Typeface provided by Adobe Systems.

Library of Congress Cataloging-in-Publication Data

Names: Johnson, Rebecca L., author. | Saroff, Phyllis V., illustrator.
Title: A walk in the desert / by Rebecca L. Johnson ; with illustrations by Phyllis V.
    Saroff.
Description: 2nd edition. | Minneapolis : Lerner Publications , [2021] | Series: Biomes
    of North America | Includes bibliographical references and index. | Audience:
    Ages 8–12 | Audience: Grades 4–6 | Summary: "From the thick green stems of
    cacti to the fluffy jackrabbits, the desert is teeming with life. Narrative text and
    you-are-there photos put the reader in the middle of this misunderstood biome
    and critical habitat"— Provided by publisher.
Identifiers: LCCN 2020034241 (print) | LCCN 2020034242 (ebook) | ISBN
    9781728429137 (library binding) | ISBN 9781728429144 (paperback) | ISBN
    9781728429151 (ebook)
Subjects: LCSH: Desert ecology—Juvenile literature. | Deserts—Juvenile literature.
Classification: LCC QH541.5.D4 J65 2021 (print) | LCC QH541.5.D4 (ebook) | DDC
    577.54—dc23

LC record available at https://lccn.loc.gov/2020034241
LC ebook record available at https://lccn.loc.gov/2020034242

Manufactured in the United States of America
1-49446-49512-8/4/2020

Words
to Know

BIOME *(BYE-ohm)*—a major community of living things that covers a large area, such as a grassland or a forest

CACTUS—a type of plant that usually grows in hot, dry places. Most cactus plants, or cacti, have thick stems that can store water. Cacti usually have sharp spines instead of leaves.

CLIMATE *(KLYE-mut)*—a region's usual pattern of weather over a long period of time

DESERT—a very dry region with rocky or sandy soil. Most deserts are very hot.

NECTAR—a sweet liquid produced by flowers. Nectar is used as food by animals such as bees, hummingbirds, and bats.

NOCTURNAL *(nahk-TUR-nuhl)*—active at night

POLLEN *(PAH-luhn)*—fine, powdery material made by flowers. Pollen is often yellow.

PREDATOR *(PREH-duh-tur)*—an animal that hunts and eats other animals

PREY *(pray)*—animals that are hunted and eaten by other animals

PUP—a baby fox

rising over the desert

Just before dawn, a kit fox pads quietly across the dry ground. She spies a kangaroo rat beneath a cactus. The fox springs—and catches her pups' next meal! She is lucky. The time for hunting has nearly ended. Sunbeams are flickering over the landscape as the sun rises. *Chuh-chuh-chuh-chuh-chuh!* The rattling call of a cactus wren breaks the silence. The fox heads for her den as another day in the desert begins.

Wind-sculpted sand dunes bake beneath a blazing sun (above). Most North American deserts are home to many kinds of living things (right).

Does the word *desert* make you think of a hot wasteland of sand? Is it a place where almost nothing lives or grows? A few deserts are like that. But most have more stones than sand. And many deserts are full of life.

Deserts are the driest places on Earth. They are found where rain is scarce and the air is very dry. In western North America, deserts stretch from Idaho south into Mexico. The largest are the Great Basin, Mojave, Sonoran, and Chihuahuan Deserts.

Biomes of North America

Arctic Ocean

Atlantic Ocean

Pacific Ocean

- tundra
- boreal forest
- deciduous forest
- temperate rain forest
- grassland
- desert
- chaparral
- tropical rain forest
- tropical scrub forest

Deserts are surrounded by other kinds of landscapes. If you travel north, you'll see grasslands and forests. North of the forests is a cold, treeless plain called the tundra. Tundra, forests, grasslands, and deserts make up Earth's main land zones. Scientists call these different land zones biomes.

Each biome has a different type of climate. The climate is an area's usual pattern of weather over a long period of time.

Every biome is home to a special group of plants. The plants are well suited to living in the biome's climate and to growing in the soil found there.

Every biome is also home to a special group of animals. In one way or another, the animals depend on the plants to survive. Many of a biome's animals eat plants. Other animals eat the plant-eaters.

Desert plants are unlike plants in any other biome. They must be able to survive with very little rain.

A coyote looks over a desert landscape where the sun is hot and water is scarce.

All the plants and animals in a biome form a community. In that community, every living thing depends on other community members for its survival. A biome's climate, soil, plants, and animals are all connected this way.

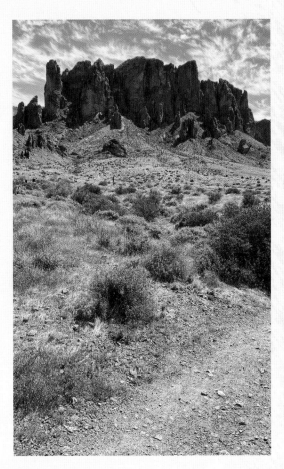

After a wet winter, spring flowers bloom (left). After a dry winter, the same patch of desert is parched and brown (below).

Deserts have a very dry climate. They do get a little rain, but it doesn't come regularly. One storm might drench a desert with several inches of rain in just a few hours. It might not rain again for months—even years.

Some deserts are cold, but most are hot. During the day, hot deserts are the hottest places on Earth. Clouds are rare in desert skies. There is nothing to block the sun's scorching rays. But when the sun goes down, deserts cool off quickly. Nighttime temperatures can be freezing cold.

It's hard to imagine that anything could live in such a harsh place. Yet most deserts are home to many living things. Let's take a walk in the desert and see what life is like here in early summer.

The landscape glows in the morning sun. You're in the middle of a rocky plain full of strange-looking plants. Many are cactus plants, or cacti. Most cacti don't have leaves. They have thick, green stems covered with sharp spines. The spines protect cacti from being eaten by desert animals. They also shade the stems from the sun.

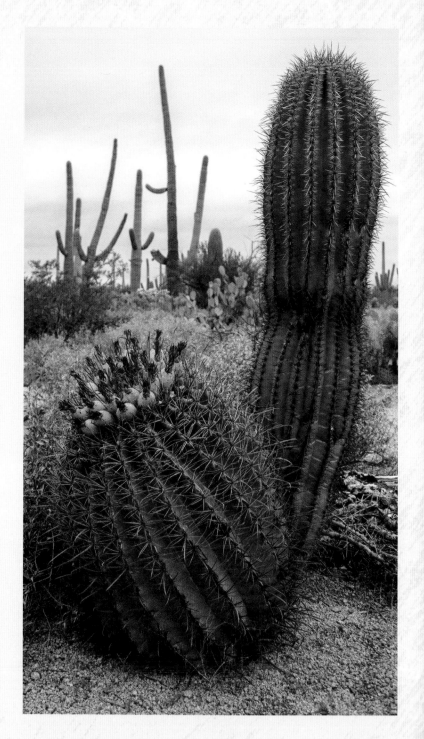

Short and squat or tall and branched, cacti are covered with spines.

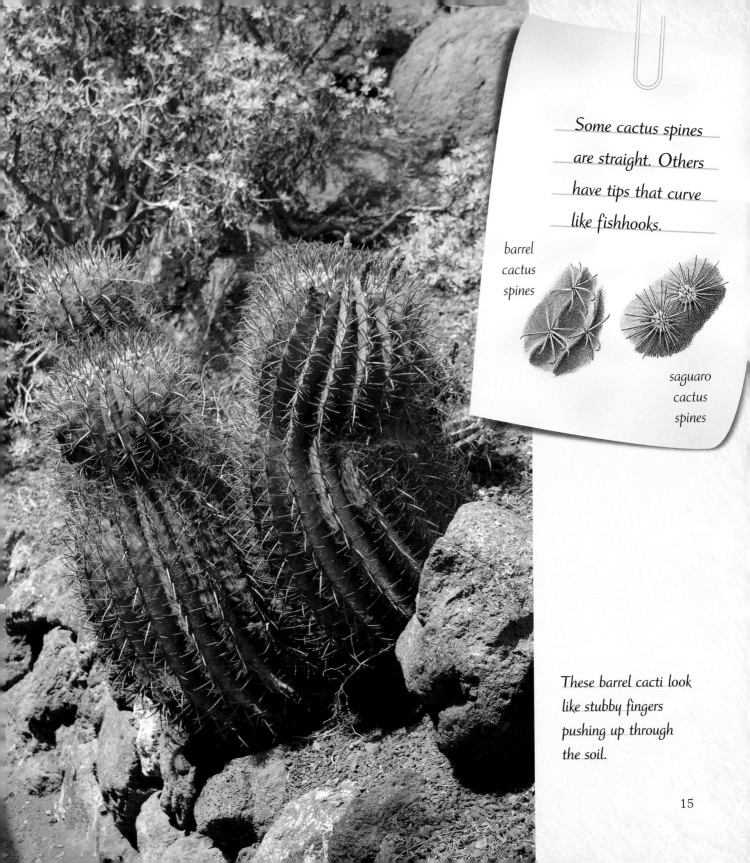

Some cactus spines are straight. Others have tips that curve like fishhooks.

barrel cactus spines

saguaro cactus spines

These barrel cacti look like stubby fingers pushing up through the soil.

15

Some cacti have so many spines, it's hard to see the green stem underneath (left).
A cholla bristles with needle-sharp spines (below).

Cacti come in many shapes and sizes. At your feet are tiny round cacti. They look like pincushions. Next to them are pancake-shaped prickly pears. Chubby barrel cacti dot the landscape. They grow about knee-high. Chollas are taller, with many spiny branches. Towering over everything are giant saguaros. They can grow as tall as a telephone pole.

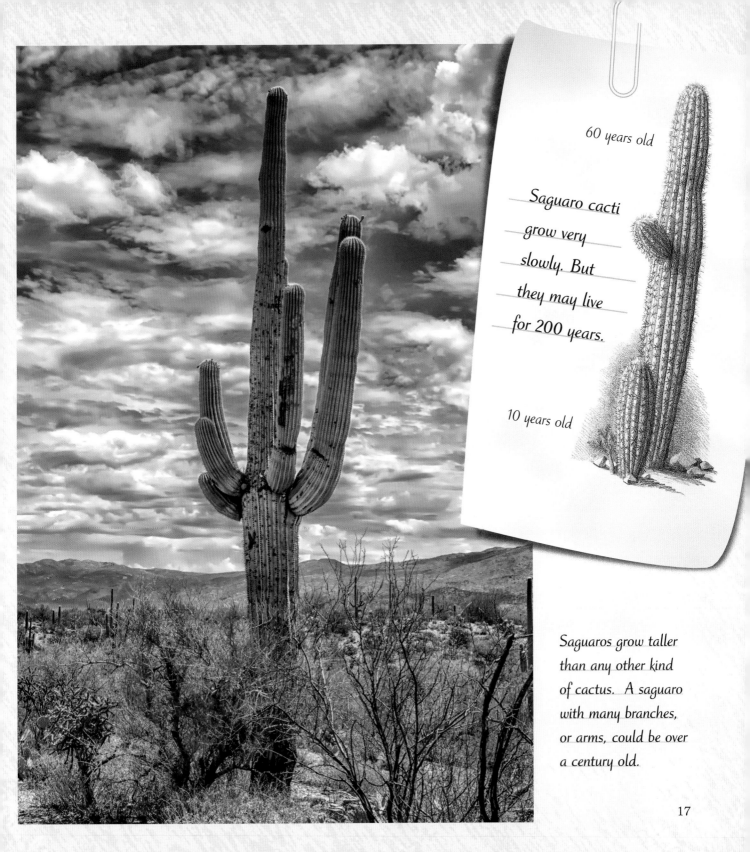

60 years old

Saguaro cacti grow very slowly. But they may live for 200 years.

10 years old

Saguaros grow taller than any other kind of cactus. A saguaro with many branches, or arms, could be over a century old.

17

The shallow roots of a barrel cactus can soak up rain as soon as it hits the ground.

Cacti store water inside their fleshy, waxy stems (above right).

Bend down and pick up a handful of soil. It's so pebbly and dry it trickles through your fingers. Desert soil contains many things that plants need to grow. But after a rain, it dries out very fast. Desert plants must be able to soak up rainwater quickly. They must save every precious drop.

Many cacti have roots that spread out just under the soil's surface. When it rains, the roots soak up the water before the soil dries out. The water is stored in a cactus's thick, fleshy stem. A waxy coating on the outside of the stem keeps the water in.

Cacti aren't the only desert plants. Creosote bushes and mesquite trees grow here, too. Both have tiny, leathery leaves. Small leaves lose less water in dry desert air than larger leaves would.

The long roots of mesquite trees tunnel deep underground to reach hidden water.

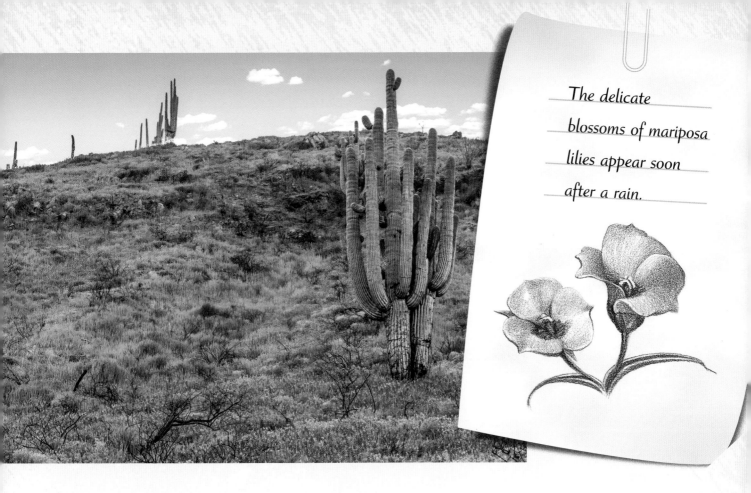

The delicate blossoms of mariposa lilies appear soon after a rain.

A spring thunderstorm soaked the desert a few weeks ago. The heavy rain woke millions of sleeping seeds. Everywhere you look, poppies, daisies, snapdragons, and other wildflowers bloom. Their bright blossoms of red, yellow, orange, and purple dance in the breeze. But in another week or two, the flowers will wither and die. Their seeds will fall to the ground. There the seeds will wait—maybe for a year or more—until heavy rains come again.

Poppies bloom on a desert hillside (left). Spring wildflowers form a colorful carpet beneath towering cacti (above left).

A cluster of beavertail cacti burst into bloom (left). *A broad-billed hummingbird sips sweet nectar from a desert wildflower* (below).

Many of the cacti are blooming, too. Bright, waxy flowers sprout from their tops and branches. Hear that buzzing and humming? Cactus flowers and wildflowers attract bees, butterflies, and wasps. Jewel-colored hummingbirds stop in midair to dip their long bills into the blossoms. All these animals drink the sweet nectar that the flowers make.

Inside the flowers are tiny, yellow grains called pollen. Pollen sticks to animals as they sip nectar. As the animals flit from flower to flower, they spread pollen from one plant to another. This process is called pollination. When plants are pollinated, they can make fruits and seeds. From seeds, new plants will grow.

A bee collects nectar from a cactus flower.

A mother desert tortoise lays her eggs in sandy soil. The sun warms the eggs until they hatch.

Desert plants provide many animals with food and water. Here comes a desert tortoise. It shuffles slowly along and stops often to rest. The tortoise stretches its long neck to nibble a wildflower. Tortoises rarely drink. They get nearly all the water they need from the plants they eat.

A desert tortoise bulldozes its way through a patch of blooming desert flowers.

Cacti also provide homes for desert animals. Halfway down a nearby saguaro's thick stem, a Gila woodpecker pecks a hole in the juicy flesh. It is making a nest for its eggs. Woodpeckers have nested in this cactus for many years, so they've made many holes in it.

A Gila woodpecker perches at the entrance to its saguaro nest.

A wood rat's nest (above right) looks like a big pile of sticks.

Other creatures have moved into some of the old woodpecker holes.

A pair of flycatchers lives in one. Another is home to a hive of honeybees. And peeking out of still another hole is an elf owl. It has white eyebrows and fierce yellow eyes.

Not far from the saguaro, you see a very different kind of desert home. Jammed between a dead cactus and a fallen tree is a huge mound of tangled twigs. It's the nest of a wood rat.

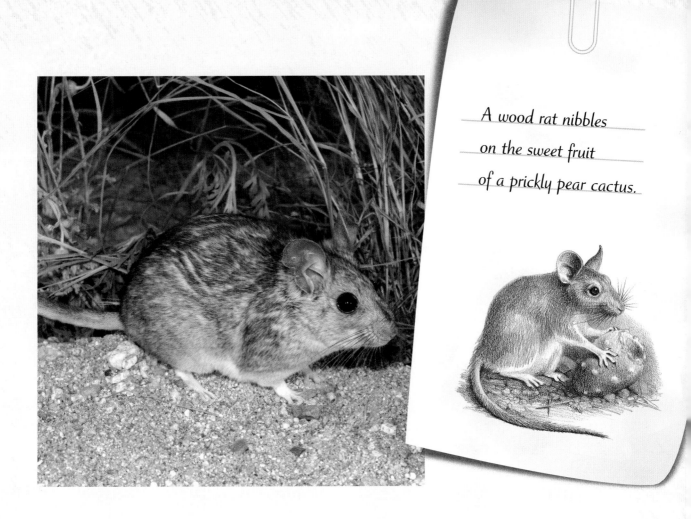

A wood rat nibbles on the sweet fruit of a prickly pear cactus.

Wood rats are also called pack rats. They use anything they can find to build enormous nests. A wood rat's nest might be made of sticks, rocks, leaves, cactus spines, or even bones. It may be as tall as a person and just as wide. The nest protects the wood rat from foxes, hawks, and other predators. It is also a cool place to hide from the hot sun.

Nose twitching, a wood rat sniffs the air to check for danger.

27

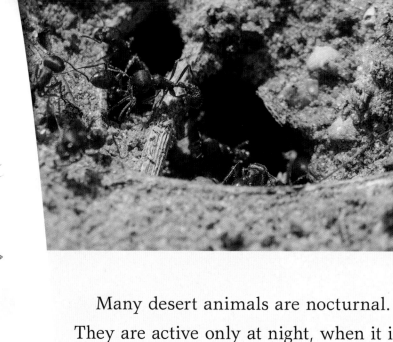

A painted grasshopper uses its long legs to hop from plant to plant—and to escape being eaten.

Ants look for food on the dry, pebbly desert ground (above right).

Many desert animals are nocturnal. They are active only at night, when it is cooler. Nocturnal desert-dwellers spend their days in burrows, dens, and other sheltered places. The kangaroo rat and the kit fox are nocturnal. They stay underground until the sun goes down.

But some desert animals are active during the day. Insects are on the move everywhere. Columns of ants march across the ground. Colorful beetles crawl up and down stems. Grasshoppers spring from leaf to leaf. Insect-eating spiders are busy, too. They spin silken webs among cactus spines.

The sun has climbed higher in the clear blue sky. Can you feel the heat? Desert lizards don't seem to mind. Their tough, scaly skin seals water inside their bodies and keeps them from drying out. Lizards rest on rocks, hunt insects, and cling to cactus stems. In one small patch of desert, you could see tiny skinks, chunky spiny-tailed iguanas, rugged horned lizards, and lumbering Gila monsters.

A horned lizard's spiny scales are a good defense against desert predators.

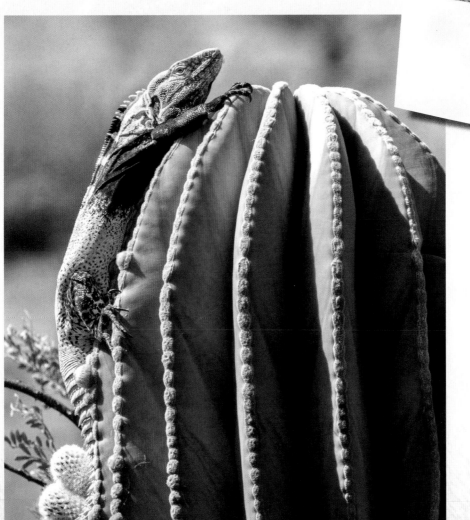

A spiny-tailed iguana atop a prickly perch soaks up the sun.

29

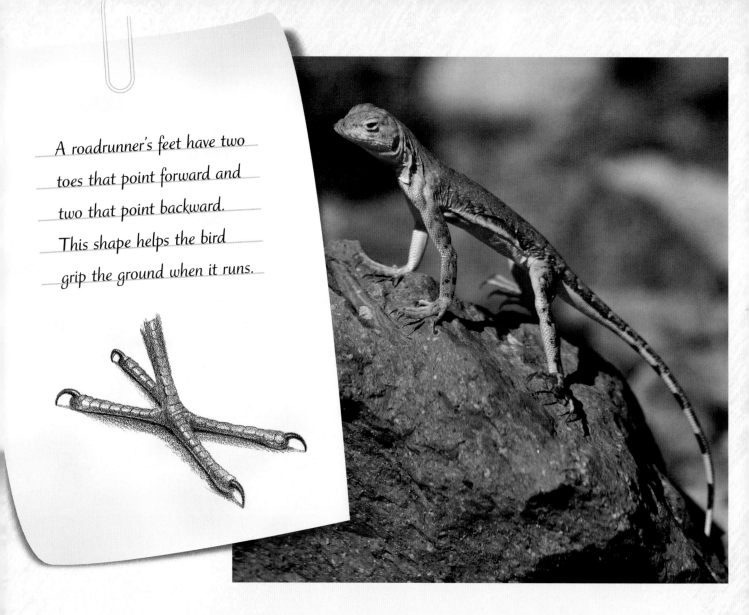

A roadrunner's feet have two toes that point forward and two that point backward. This shape helps the bird grip the ground when it runs.

With long legs and a slim body, the zebra-tailed lizard (above right) is built for speed.

Suddenly, something streaks across your path. It's a speedy lizard, and right on its heels is a roadrunner. Roadrunners can fly. But these desert birds prefer to run after lizards and the other small animals they hunt.

Roadrunners have long, strong legs. They can run as fast as many lizards can. In fact, this time the bird is faster. The roadrunner catches the lizard by its tail and swallows it in one gulp.

A roadrunner snares dinner in its sturdy beak.

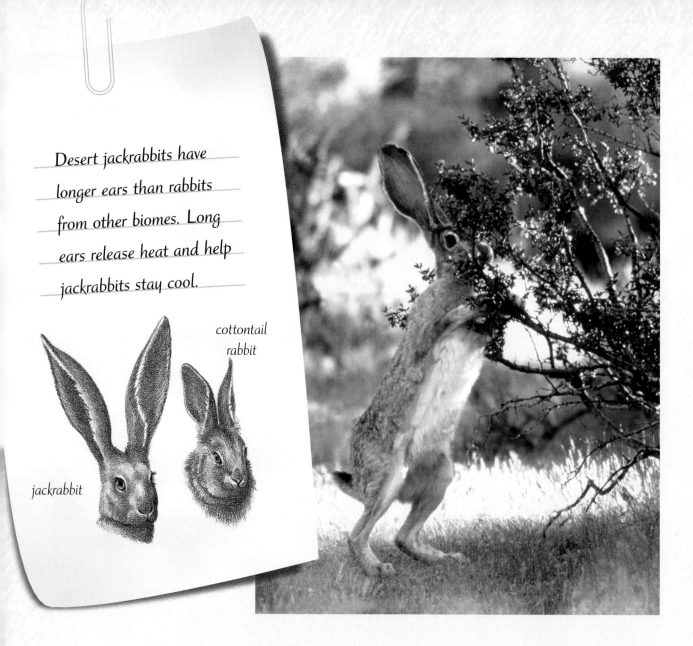

Desert jackrabbits have longer ears than rabbits from other biomes. Long ears release heat and help jackrabbits stay cool.

cottontail rabbit

jackrabbit

A black-tailed jackrabbit dines on tender leaves (above right).

Nearby, a jackrabbit looks for plants to nibble. Jackrabbits are even faster than roadrunners. They can outrun almost everything in the desert. They can even outrun coyotes—most of the time!

Coyotes eat rabbits when they can catch them. But they will eat just about anything, from birds and lizards to berries. To find underground water, they dig holes in dry streambeds. Coyotes can survive almost anywhere.

By noon, even the coyotes are panting. It's well over 100 degrees. The sun is a fireball overhead. Nearly all the daytime animals move into the shade of rocks and cacti during the hottest part of the day.

A coyote slips quietly among bushes as it hunts.

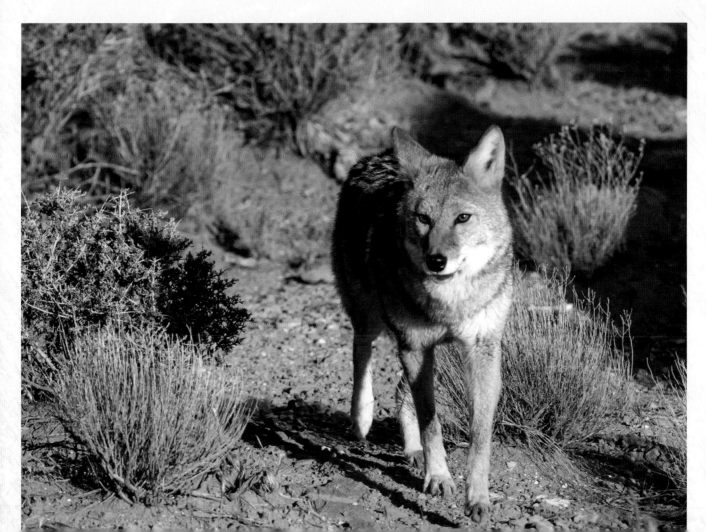

A mother scorpion carries her babies around on her back until they can survive on their own.

Take a tip from the animals. Find a place out of the sun to rest. Just be careful where you sit. Scorpions often lurk in crevices or under rocks during the day. A scorpion's tail has a stinger filled with poison. Few kinds of scorpions can kill a person. But the sting of any scorpion is very painful.

A scorpion uses its large pincers to catch spiders and other small prey. Its stinger is used mostly for defense.

A rattlesnake's rattle is made up of a row of large, dry scales.

Watch out for hiding rattlesnakes and coral snakes, too. Their poison is deadly. You don't want to get within striking distance of either one.

Heat waves shimmer above the landscape. The leaves of the mesquite trees curl up. Curled leaves lose less water to the hot, dry air. The desert is very quiet. Most of the birds are silent. They seem to be waiting for the sun's fierce heat to fade.

Coiled like a spring, a diamondback rattlesnake is ready to strike (above left).

The sun slips below the horizon as the desert night begins.

Gradually, the sun moves lower in the sky. As shadows grow longer, the temperature starts to drop. Desert birds begin to sing again. At sunset, coyotes call to each other, barking and yelping. They join voices in an eerie, wailing song.

The hot desert day is over. The cool night is about
to begin. Birds, lizards, and other daytime animals
retreat to snug nests and safe hiding places. There
they will sleep the night away. As darkness falls, the
nocturnal animals begin to stir.

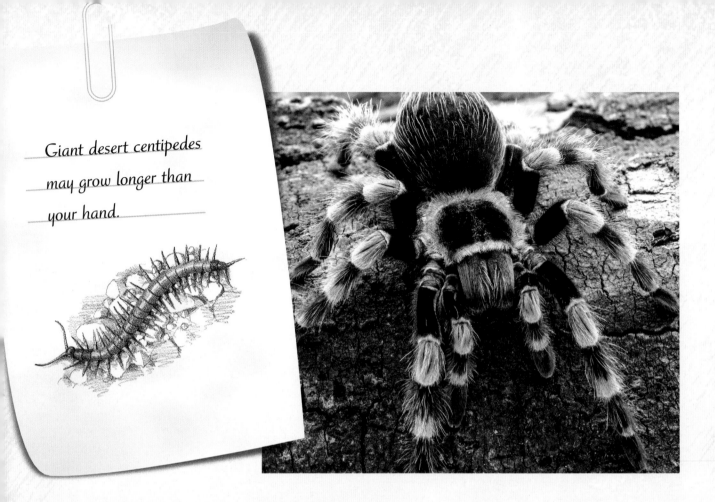

Giant desert centipedes may grow longer than your hand.

Tarantulas (above right) are some of the largest spiders in the world.

Snakes slither into the open. They are ready to track down rats, rabbits, and birds that nest on the ground. Scorpions scuttle around. They search for crickets, spiders, and small, sleeping lizards. Many-legged centipedes crawl out from nooks and crannies to hunt insects.

Hairy tarantulas creep out of holes in the ground. They look scary. But they are dangerous only to the insects and other small creatures they eat.

Bats flutter out of caves. They look like dark shadows against the night sky. Some seek the sweet nectar of cactus flowers. Others hunt for flying insects.

A Mexican long-nosed bat flies in to sip nectar from a saguaro flower.

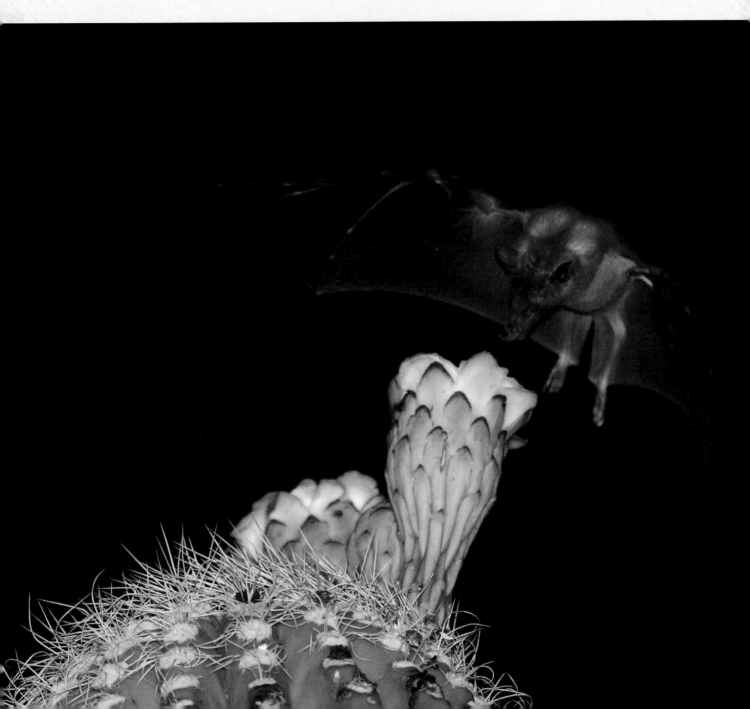

Constantly alert for danger, a kangaroo rat stuffs its cheek pouches with seeds.

An elf owl whistles softly as it flies out from its saguaro hotel. It glides silently through the cool night air. The owl dives to the ground to catch a small snake in its sharp claws.

Up from their burrows come kangaroo rats. All night they bound around on long hind legs, noses twitching, searching for seeds. Wood rats also leave their nests to look for food. Kit foxes quietly stalk rats and mice, and maybe a sleeping roadrunner, too.

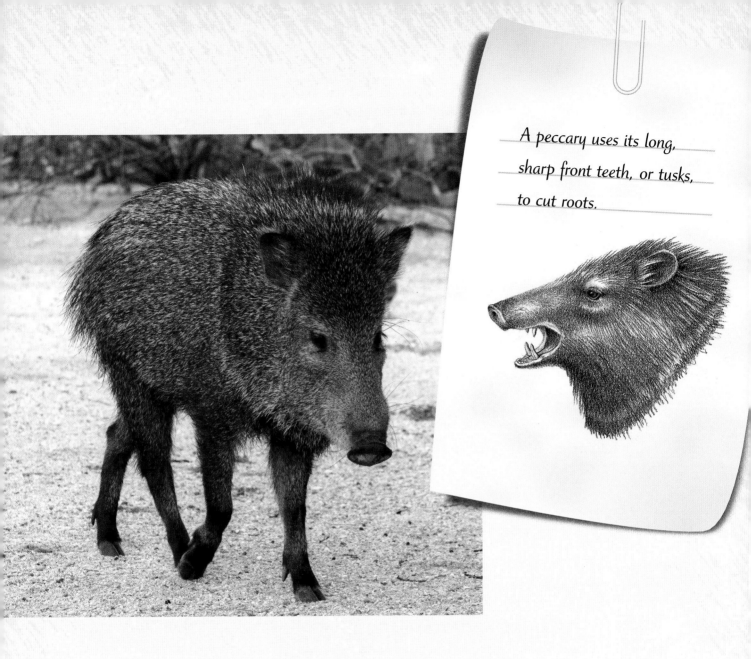

A peccary uses its long, sharp front teeth, or tusks, to cut roots.

Wait—hear that? Soft grunting sounds are coming from a clump of creosote bushes. There's a strong musky odor in the air, too. Peccaries are near. Peccaries are piglike animals with coarse, bristly hair.

Peccaries are also called by their Spanish name, javelina.

41

During the day, peccaries sleep in the shade. But at night, they travel in noisy groups. They poke the dry soil with their long snouts, eating roots and tender plants. One of their favorite foods is prickly pear cactus. Peccaries don't seem to mind the prickly pear's sharp spines.

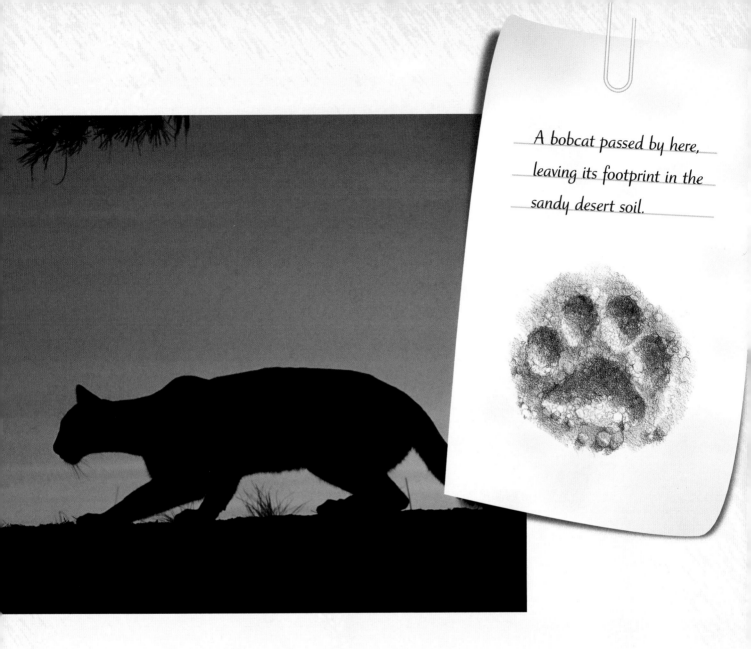

A bobcat passed by here, leaving its footprint in the sandy desert soil.

The scent of peccaries can attract large desert hunters. Bobcats and mountain lions hide in the shadows, waiting for animals to pass by. Then, in a flash, they spring out and pounce on their prey.

Sleek and powerful, a mountain lion begins its nightly search for food.

On cold nights, desert birds stay warm by fluffing up their feathers.

As the hours pass, the cool night air turns cold. The temperature may drop 60 degrees or more between sunset and sunrise. The fur coats of foxes, bobcats, and rats protect them from the cold. Owls have fluffy feathers to keep them warm.

All night long, the desert is a busy place. It is full of slithering, rustling, whispering sounds as animals move about. By the light of the stars and the moon, they fly and hop and run and pounce.

At dawn, the branches of a Joshua tree stand out against the glowing sky.

44

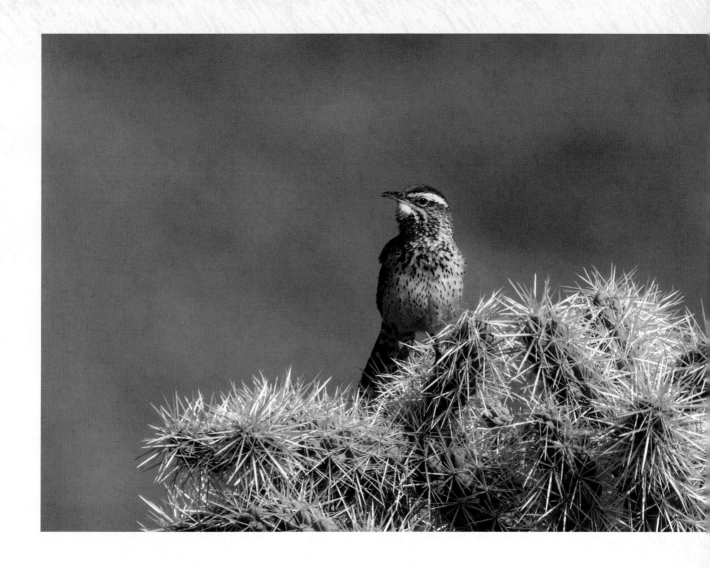

Eventually, the rosy glow of dawn lights up the eastern sky. Owls and bats return to their roosts. Kit foxes and kangaroo rats retreat to underground burrows. Snakes and scorpions go back into hiding, too. And when the cactus wren calls out at sunrise, the cycle of life in the desert begins all over again.

Perched on a cholla, a cactus wren welcomes a new day in the desert.

Deserts in Danger

Human activities are changing climates worldwide. Vehicles, factories, and homes release greenhouse gases into Earth's atmosphere. These gases trap heat rising from the planet's sun-warmed surface. Climate change is making some deserts hotter and drier, and survival in these biomes is more difficult.

As the climate changes, so do desert plants. Wildflowers don't bloom as often. With less rain, scorching wildfires are more common. Slower-growing trees and cacti give way to faster-growing grasses.

With fewer trees and cacti to provide shade, some animals can't escape the desert heat. Other animals struggle to find enough water. Water holes that appear after rains don't last as long as they once did.

You can help save deserts by fighting climate change. Reduce greenhouse gases by turning off lights and unplugging devices when you aren't using them. Such simple actions can help cacti and kit foxes and all the other plants and animals for which deserts are home.

for further
Information
about the Desert

Cocca, Lisa Caolozza. *Desert Animals*.
Vero Beach, FL: Rourke, 2020.

Kids Do Ecology—Desert
http://kids.nceas.ucsb.edu/biomes/desert
.html

Markle, Sandra. *Locusts: An Augmented
Reality Experience*. Minneapolis: Lerner
Publications, 2021.

McPartland, Lisa A. *Changing Desert
Environments*. New York: PowerKids
Press, 2020.

San Diego Zoo Animals & Plants—Desert
https://animals.sandiegozoo.org/habitats
/desert

Shoals, James. *The Vital Role of Deserts
and Forests*. Broomall, PA: Mason Crest,
2020.

Sonoran Desert Plants and Wildlife
https://www.inaturalist.org/guides/2488

World Wildlife Fund—Deserts
https://www.worldwildlife.org/habitats
/deserts

Photo Acknowledgments

Image credits: Max Allen/Shutterstock.com, pp. 4-5;
Mirigrina/Shutterstock.com, p. 6; Charles T. Peden/
Shutterstock.com, pp. 7, 25, 41; Amy Newton
-McConnel/Shutterstock.com, p. 9; Joe Cramer/
Shutterstock.com, p. 10; Shandraz/Shutterstock.com,
pp. 11 (left, right); aleksander hunta/Shutterstock
.com, p. 12; Clinton Harris/Shutterstock.com, p. 13;
Nate Hovee/Shutterstock.com, p. 14; Peter Etchells/
Shutterstock.com, p. 15; Marc Venema/Shutterstock
.com, p. 16 (top left); Wildnerdpix/Shutterstock.com,
p. 16 (bottom right); Anna Krivitskaya/Shutterstock
.com, p. 17; david n madden/Shutterstock.com,
p. 18; EuToch/Getty Images, p. 19; Monica Lara/
Shutterstock.com, pp. 20, 21; Dominic Gentilcore
PhD/Shutterstock.com, p. 22 (left); Hal Beral/Corbis/
Getty Images, p. 22 (right); JRosamond/Shutterstock.
com, p. 23; Design Pics/David Ponton/Getty Images,
p. 24; Janzig/USA/Alamy Stock Photo, p. 26; Rick &
Nora Bowers/Alamy Stock Photo, p. 27; thamerpic/
Getty Images, p. 28; Danita Delimont/Alamy
Stock Photo, p. 29; D. A. Boyd/Shutterstock
.com, p. 30; SumikoPhoto/Getty Images, p. 31; Terry
W. Eggers/Getty Images, p. 32; Warren Metcalf/
Shutterstock.com, p. 33; IrinaK/Shutterstock
.com, p. 34; Alexander Wong/Shutterstock.com,
p. 35; Gill Couto/Shutterstock.com, pp. 36-37;
Ernie Cooper/Shutterstock.com, p. 38; SearchNet
Media/Moment Open/Getty Images, p. 39; Nicholas
Taffs/Shutterstock.com, p. 40; Igor Pushkarev/
Shutterstock.com, p. 42; Chase Swift/The Image
Bank/Getty Images, p. 43; kesterhu/Shutterstock
.com, p. 44; Dee Carpenter Originals/Shutterstock
.com, p. 45.

Front cover: Melinda Fawver/Shutterstock
.com, Steve Bower/Shutterstock.com. Back cover:
Melchakov/Shutterstock.com.

Index

Numbers in **bold** refer to photos and drawings